Nature in Maine

Thoughts from My Life in the Wild

by

Gary W. Fogg

Contents

Introduction

Wildlife as Neighbors

South of Bangor

Introduction

The purpose of this book is to celebrate nature as I have found it in Maine. Since the land and wildlife here have been highly altered by development over four centuries, I am writing about a world where wild nature has survived in a diminished form unique to our time. It is beautiful and resurgent but not pristine and not the same as it was before Europeans arrived. All of the facts I present are true based on my own experience and research. Every event I describe I have done or witnessed myself during my journeys on foot or by canoe. The selections are short and somewhat philosophical. That is because I endeavor to say a lot in few words. The book is organized into five main themes about nature and these in turn are organized into smaller groups of related subjects. There are just over one hundred selections in all. They are intended to be easy to read and understand and I hope that my countrymen find them inspiring and informative.

Introduction

Landscapes

1. Fields

Perspective

Among the woods of Midcoast Maine are fields
exposed to light and air. The fields follow the
form of the land, rolling up and down over hills
and swales. In spring and summer flowers wave
among the grass until the fields are hayed or
grazed by sheep and cattle. I love these fields as
well as the forest. Not only are they beautiful but
they help us to see the world in perspective. When
the distance we see is far, then we know how large
or small our problems are.

Salt Hay

Salt meadows were once a part of every farm
along the coast. The meadows were flooded by the
tides each month and what the tides yielded was a
stiff green grass about one foot high. In the early
days before the forests were cleared, salt meadow
cord grass, as it is called, was the only hay for
livestock available. Farmers praised it for keeping
their animals healthy and hardy. Even after fields
on the uplands were cleared and planted with
timothy and clover, farmers still cut extra hay

1

from the marsh because no money or work was required to plant it. Thus, farmers turned wetlands to advantage and harvested their crops in harmony with the tides as well as the seasons.

Fences

The fences that enclose these fields stretch onward through brush and flowers past open woods and clusters of boulders. They travel over brooks and ditches and sometimes enter the water of small streams and rivers. Fences tell us a lot about the character of a farm and the men and women who own it. For people who make a living by grassland farming, the fences tell us just how well or poorly the farmers are doing.

Hobby Farms

The little farms are cozy and welcoming. Dogs and cats mingle with chickens in the barnyard and donkeys protect sheep in the fields from coyotes. The fields are not large but they are wondrously welcome in this land overrun by highways and buildings. The owners take great care to keep their animals happy, so the sheds and barns come in all shapes and sizes. Even the character of the fields vary like their owners. Some are green and manicured like a lawn. Others are wild and bushy. Either way, these little farms reflect the best effort of their owners to keep their dream of a country life going.

2. Flowers

Mallow

I first encountered mallows in these fields when I was young. The burst of lavender petals among the high grass along the roadside and the hedgerows early in summer caught me by surprise. It wasn't just the color that endeared me to them so strongly, but the fact that they existed at all. For one who worked long hours on a turkey farm devoted to slaughter, to come across fields filled with these flowers was momentous. In my mind I asked, "Is nature always this beautiful and mankind always this ugly?"

Spikelets

When I first discovered flowers, I began to understand why they have succeeded so well on this planet. Even grasses, sedges and rushes have small flowers called spikelets with intriguing little parts, colors and textures. The spikelets are arranged on the stems of the plants in all kinds of ways. Some stand up like miniature fir trees and others hang down like the hair on my head.

Patterns like these make it easy for the wind to move pollen among them. No wonder flowering plants do so well and provide us humans though we do not deserve it with so much food, joy and forgiveness.

Oak and Maple

The flowers of oak trees are yellow-green and those of red maple are scarlet or purple. They are so common among hardwoods in spring they create a flourish of color that rivals the leaves of the forest in autumn. The flowers are small, it is true, but they are more effervescent. They make the forest glow among the gray bark of tree limbs and the gray skies of wet weather. When the showers in spring are over, these flowers give life to a world that is hungry and tired.

Canada Mayflower

White pine are the biggest trees in Maine and in old stands they dwarf every other plant in the forest. Nonetheless, among the pine needles on the forest floor are tiny plants with two green leaves called Canada mayflowers. The flowers make a living from the acid soil and the dappled light that moves over the ground from morning to evening. In nature, wherever there is something quite large there will also be something quite small. And so it is that plants as different as white pine trees and Canada mayflowers grow side by side harmoniously. By striving to do what each does best they make the world better for all of us.

3. Light and Color

Green

Water and sediment from six rivers flowing together on Merrymeeting Bay create wetlands of many kinds and sizes. There are sandbar forests of silver maple and green ash, stands of wild rice in shallow water and winding creeks lined with soft-stem rushes and yellow waterlilies. On higher ground are lovely wet meadows of blue joint grass and shrublands composed of willows and viburnums. In June when the plants in all of these wetlands turn green the color is stunning. Over the years, encountering the color green this way has affected me deeply and from this experience I have learned to love the bay more than ever.

Petals

From a flower's point of view, the primary task of primates like ourselves is to eat the fruit they produce and then disperse the seeds by swinging through the trees or walking through the landscape. Our way of seeing has, therefore, evolved to see the bright colors that fruit possess. In contrast, what matters most to flowers before the fruit appears are pollinators like moths and bees. That is because these small creatures unlike ourselves see well in ultraviolet. To them the petals of flowers bear designs like the circles on a target or the lights on a runway. The patterns lead the insects to the nectar within, a nutritious gift the flowers offer for the service insects provide in transporting pollen from one flower to another. People say that in nature all is fierce competition, but as flowering plants show this is not the whole story. In the real world, not the one we imagine, many species cooperate for the benefit of all.

Meaning

The world appears differently to us depending on how light reveals or obscures its color, form and meaning. With this in mind, we can study how backlighting delineates form, how light diffused by high clouds or fog eliminates shadows, and how the sun when low in the sky illuminates space and distance. Light changes with the weather, the time of day and the season, so we must pay close attention to nature to gain this knowledge. The effort is worthwhile, because to understand light is to understand what makes the world beautiful.

4. Mountains

Summit

Leaning into the wind, my weight upon the poles, I hold my arms close to my chest. The gear I have on will not retain my warmth for long against a wind as cold as this. But I can stay awhile, gazing in pure delight upon the sky above and the forest below. White drifts and bare rock alternate on the mountain tops. The valleys are covered in snow. The beauty of these mountains in winter and the roar of the wind are comforting to me. I wish only to be present here, to be fully aware in the wilderness. Leaning into the wind, I feel the cold creeping into my clothes, but I can last a little longer gazing on contentedly.

Rain

Forest trees hold the rainfall back. Water adheres to twigs and bark, to stumps and leaves. So much water seeps into the ground it raises the level of the streams. It takes a lot of water to make a forest grow, so a storm is a good time to see things from the forest's point of view. Roaring winds and clattering tree limbs keep us alert as we hike through.

Snow

I stride through the hills on snowshoes with ease. The cold air and snow are restful and pure. I travel at will and as far as I please. No riches compare to hiking in winter when the snow is soft and deep. I float over its surface like a bird in the air, no strain on my feet. Such comfort is rare even here in the woods. Surely in winter the hiking is good.

Bald Head

We hike to Bald Head from the shore of the Kennebec River over an old farm road covered in snow. Slabs of ice piled high on the riverbank reflect light into the forest, making the tree bark glow. From the top of the mountain, the view is grand. The great river sparkling in the sun flows restlessly to the sea, rimmed by marshes and tidal flats and surrounded by high hills. The vista from Bald Head is beautiful at any time of year, but only in winter do snow and ice make this lonely world so dazzling.

Noble Life

The spruce on the mountainside creak as the cold wind blows and snow flies over ledges and cliffs. Tufts of gray and white cloud collide with the summit. This mountain in winter is beautiful, cold and stark. It does not care whether I live or die and it does not strive to control my thoughts and feelings. This mountain's indifference to my fate is more welcoming to me than civilization with all of its greed and lies. I am happy here. The solitude is sublime and life without killing is noble.

Symbols

The mountains rise from the land around them like giants. Their armor is quartzite and hardened conglomerates. These hard stones shield the mountains for awhile from the force of freezing rain and ice that splits bare rock and grinds it to dust and gravel. The land around the mountains has washed away, but the mountains still tower above us shrouded in mist. They are sacred to us because of their size and wildness, but also because they have survived in spite of man. In their lonely existence they symbolize freedom.

Water

In spring and fall hard rains and mist keep water falling over fern-covered ledges and cliffs. Even in summer, when the weather is dry, water in stream beds still seeps beneath the gravel and boulders. A single storm will make these brooks roar again. We owe the mountains more than we think. They reach into the sky and wring moisture from the clouds, giving us water to drink and filling our lakes and rivers.

Kings

We follow the trail to the summit. We rest at our leisure among the rocks and ledges. Whether the day is warm or cold, we find solace here. We come not just for the thrill of hiking upward into the sky, as fun as that is, but also to see what the world looks like from a distance. We are surprised by how beautiful it appears. All that bothered us down below has vanished into a lovely pattern of villages, woods and meadows. For a moment we are kings of all we survey, for who can say no to our imaginings?

5. Rocks

Schist

Climbing over the mounds of schist on the shore of coastal Maine is like climbing over knives. The thin bands of shining gray rock lay upended on their side. The hapless child and the unwary adult walk gingerly over this battlefield in bare feet. Old men like me wear boots instead or sandals with thick soles like Roman legionnaires once did. The schist was formed from mud once lying at the

bottom of an ancient sea. A lot has happened since
then and now these sharp rocks do not feel like
mud to me.

Gneiss

It looks like granite but its a metamorphic rock.
So it was made from other kinds of stone. The
bands of light and dark, which may be subtle,
show how heat and pressure realigned the
minerals. On gneiss you never know what you
might be walking on. It could be an old sea floor
or lava from deep within the earth, but either way,
through the magic of change, you get a very hard
stone along the shore that can sink a ship or
provide a child with endless pleasure.

Granite

Here in coastal Maine some people call every rock
a piece of granite. Of course that isn't so, but it is
true that in some places granite is the only rock
you will find on an island or a hill. Its not that
nature likes granite more than other kinds of
stone. Its just that granite takes longer to wear
down, break apart and become mud in the bays.
Besides, it splits into useful shapes like cubes and
prisms, and so not only do we find this speckled
gray and white rock along the shore and mountain

11

tops but also in our public buildings, walls and patios.

Basalt

There is a rock along the coast that arrived a long time ago as molten lava squeezed like putty into the cracks among other types of stone. Today these roots of ancient lava flows are all that's left beating back waves along the shore. They form columns and pillars stained brown from rust for they are rich in iron. Some lean over the water like eagles searching for prey. Others crumble into piles of debris heaped up by surf. A great coast ought to have great cliffs and basalt is a rock downeast that plays this role splendidly.

6. Seaside Forest

Oaks

Among the spruce and fir in Maine oak trees are common, especially on rocky slopes where the sun is warm and the soil is dry and shallow. But perhaps where we are most likely to notice them from a distance is where the forest has been cleared for houses, roads and villages. People find oaks useful for shade around their homes among other things. Indeed, along the coast as we approach the shore from the open water, one of the first signs of mankind we observe are the broad green leaves of oak trees waving in the breeze and glistening in the sunlight.

White Birch

The white birch is one of several broad-leaved trees that live in forests of spruce and fir. Their presence in large numbers tell us that the forest has been disturbed. The main causes in the past were logging, wind and fire. The logging is shown by old stumps rotting on the forest floor. The wind is shown by old root mounds covered in lichen. The fire is shown by ashes and charcoal beneath the mulch and leaves. Every species in the forest tells a story. In the spruce-fir woods of Maine, white birch trees tell a story of sudden change.

Blowdowns

On islands along the coast spruce and fir are falling down. They fall in heaps one upon another or in rows all pointed in one direction. But under the mounds of debris and the canopy of birch trees shooting up overhead are thousands of tiny spruce and fir seeking light and air. The trees falling down grew back on old pastures when farming on the islands was abandoned. Now the wind with the aid of shallow soil is clearing the forest again.

Cycles are the norm in nature and though these spruce and fir are small right now they will soon tower into the sky once more.

Friends

Shrubs and flowers along the shore in Midcoast Maine grow in bands or rows. The pattern depends on factors like salt spray, how deep the soil is and access to sunlight. On sandy shores exposed to waves and flooding, beach grass and wild radish are common. On rocky ledges swept by the wind, seaside plantain and seaside goldenrod cling to bits of soil trapped in crevices. Next to the woods where the soils are deeper but sunlight is still abundant many kinds of shrubs take over. Rosa rugosa is prickly. Huckleberry turns red in the fall. Bayberry is used for candles. The flowers on all these species and many others are often pink and yellow but red and white are also common. Different flowers come and go as the weeks pass by but some are always there in summer. In Midcoast Maine one gets to know the shrubs and flowers that grow by the water. As we paddle near shore they are like friends coming out to greet us.

7. Soil

Moisture

No real soil exists in coastal Maine. What we have instead are ledges, rocks and gravel. I am not complaining, mind you. We need something to stand and walk upon while we make a living and what we have is fairly solid. Its just that I don't pretend we have any soil fit for farming. We quarry stone in places, dig sand and gravel in others, but growing crops in long rows isn't much of an option. So it might come as a surprise to learn that the coast is actually quite good for growing small gardens. That's because instead of soil we have lots of rain and fog. All that water keeps the gardens thriving. People must do their best with what they have and along the coast what we have is moisture.

Knee High Forest

In Midcoast Maine are sand plains with forests of pine, spruce and oak. The sand was laid down in deep water near shore when the last glacier retreated. Now that the land has risen above sea level, it has a characteristic look caused by its flatness and the plants that flourish there. On sand plains today that have not yet been developed, the forest is stunning. Sunlight streams through the canopy of big trees and among the shadows and patches of light on the forest floor is another forest in miniature. It is only knee high, a world where bracken, blueberries and sheep laurel hover above diminutive shrubs like dewberries and wintergreen. In every season new life appears. Small birds and mammals forage among the twigs and leaves even in winter. One never knows how great events in the world's history will affect life in the future. Although the glaciers that covered this continent with ice and snow are gone, the sand they left behind keeps these tiny forests growing.

Talus Slopes

On mountains in Maine are hillsides covered in boulders and heaps of rock. The stones on these talus slopes have been plucked from the mountainside by glaciers or split off cliffs by ice and cold. To the trees that grow in wild places, even these heaps of stone are good habitat. The trees send their roots down into the leaf mold and gravel trapped among the stones. Nutrients concentrate there from decaying plant matter and water seeps down through the rocks from rainfall. Thus, the trees grow well even though no soil as we define it is present. In nature, plants find many ways to overcome hardships. On talus slopes, they thrive by taking advantage of cracks in the system. Let this be a lesson for all who love nature and freedom.

People and Places

1. Acadia

Grassy Knoll

We were hiking at Acadia one calm and balmy spring morning when we stopped upon a grassy knoll. What better way, we thought, to spend a minute or two gazing upon the mountains above and the beach below. We took out our books and began to read, taking note from time to time of the light as the sun passed overhead and puffy white clouds sailed quietly over the Beehive and its cliffs. While we were thus engaged, animals came and went. A snowshoe hare hopped out to graze, a fox trotted by, crows landed in the trees, a goshawk passed overhead and squirrels foraged among the leaves. We took notice of each visitor as it arrived but did not interfere. We had lots of other things to do, like books to read, clouds to watch and surf that we could listen to. Gradually time passed and we realized that the sun was now setting in the west behind Champlain Mountain. We noticed that the gulls and eiders who had been hunting all day on the waves near shore had flown away and that even the crows in the woods had left. But while the birds were retiring for the night, mammals like bats, beaver, mice and deer were just emerging to forage in the woods and meadows. We took the darkness as a cue to leave. We had been lounging on the knoll from dawn until sunset. It had been, we said, a very good day.

Clearings

We came upon small clearings while hiking at Acadia one spring. Deer had browsed the birch and poplar so well that we could walk through these groves of trees without stooping to avoid twigs and branches. Sunlight filtered down through the partial canopy of leaves and the ground was covered with grass and flowers. We sat down upon a rock to meditate on what these clearings could mean. The birch and poplar, we knew, arrived many years before when fire consumed the spruce and fir. The heat and ashes prepared the soil for grass and flowers. Rain and sunlight made the grass and flowers grow. For decades after that the deer kept these lovely park-like settings open by grazing and browsing. The clearings reminded us of the meadows out west maintained by elk and bison. They showed just how well herbivores even here in Maine can manage a forest when they are given a little help now and then from fire. After thoughts like these we got up from our rock and continued our hike across the mountain ridges and valleys. We found many things in which we took delight, but the sunny groves of birch and poplar remained special in our thoughts and feelings. When love of nature runs deep, we never know what we will see and learn as we saunter through the forest.

2. Artifacts

Rubble

The rubble the glaciers left behind in Maine consists of stones, coarse gravel and sand. Railroad companies once filled ravines and waterways with this rubble to lay their tracks. Merchants once used this rubble to build piers for sailing ships and steamers. Farmers once pushed this rubble aside to plow their fields. Today, the rubble the glaciers left behind is still mined for things we want to do, but we use so much of it that even what the glaciers left is not always enough. To make the world smooth and safe for automobiles, we level the hills and fill the valleys too. I prefer the landscape that the glaciers made. Rubble dammed the streams to make ponds and lakes for fish. Rubble made farmland from plains of sand and silt. Rubble created the soil and heaps of rock on which our forests grow. The rugged land the glaciers left behind was wild and beautiful. It was filled with life, and nature, like a promise of redemption, still thrives wherever fragments of this glacier made world are left.

Towers

Almost every high hill in Maine where a wealthy town once stood had a tower. The towers were built before the days of the automobile, when people made a living from farming, manufacturing and sailing around the world. They used their modest wealth to build these towers to get a view of where they lived. What they saw were small towns surrounded by fields, forests on distant mountainsides and the sea speckled with vessels under sail. The perfect hill had a steep side to improve the view and a gradual one for a carriage road to the top. Hotels were built on some where railroads and steamboats brought customers in to the valleys below. Today the towers and hotels are nearly all gone and the forest has grown back where the fields were once mowed. Even so, the stone foundations of the buildings are still there among tree trunks and leaves. What we learn in these woods is that if people have money to spare, they seek to do more than work. They enhance their lives by climbing hills and looking at the world in ways they never did before.

Pilings

If trees fall in the forest, the part that touches the ground rots first. The opposite is true when trees along the coast are sunk into the mud for piers and docks. That is why we come across old pilings in the mud that are well preserved. These pilings are relics of the sailing and steamboat era, when almost every hamlet and village along the coast built ships on ways along the shore or welcomed steamboats at piers stretched far out into deep water. Travel by sea before the days of the automobile was the norm, even after the railroads were built. It was not so long ago, yet the docks and steamboats are all gone. This was the world without cars my grandparents knew. They were middle class. They came and went on steamboats as they pleased. On vacation they rowed small skiffs and paddled canoes. They picked blueberries on rocky fields with magnificent views. They read books. They had full lives and discussed ideas in depth. When I think of my grandparents, I think of how they made a living here and had a good life. The automobile swept this world away. Now we live among highways and shopping malls. What we have lost among other things is silence and time for pondering.

Elm Trees

The elm tree plan for survival can be described like this:

Spread seed on the wind late in the spring after the poplars and willows. Germinate quickly on soil moistened by rain or floods. Grow well under the shade of other trees, then overtop them and grow even faster under full sun. Spread branches outward to increase sunlight on the leaves and shade competing trees underneath. Live a long life like this alone or in small stands of other elms as a big tree in the woods.

This strategy ensured that elms on this continent survived for eons in great numbers. Elms grew so fast and large that Anglo-Americans even planted them on lawns and next to city streets. But then the Anglo-Americans caused a wrinkle in the elm tree plan. From Europe they brought without intent a disease for which the elms had no defense. Undone by this folly, big elms succumbed. Surely the elm tree plan for survival was put to the test. Though elms today have disappeared from lawns and city streets, young elms not yet infected with disease still thrive in our floodplains by rivers and streams. They spread seed to the wind each spring and the seed still grows in the fresh soil where elms have always done best. These young elms do not survive to become old and dominate trees, but their presence in the forest keeps the species going. They give us hope that one day these magnificent trees will tower over the land once more.

3. Hunter-gatherers

Culture

There was a time when people in Maine were few in number and made a living from our waterways without harming them. They were hunters to be sure, but the water remained clean and wildlife flourished. They harvested fish, seals, reptiles and birds according to the season in which each was most abundant. This avoided overuse and left the world beautiful in spite of the killing. Like other species, they were part of the system and met all of their needs from the bounty Maine offered.

Stone Traps

Where rivers and streams rise and fall with the tides along the coast we can find low berms of stones crossing the mouths of creeks and the narrows between islands and the mainland shore. These berms look like windrows of hay raked up by farmers in a field or heaps of wrack tossed upon a beach by waves. But the stones in these berms were carried there by hand and placed carefully to trap fish. How effective these traps are we can see for ourselves, for when the tide is going out and the water is low fish are trapped in pools or squeezed through chutes where they are easily caught in nets or speared.

Middens

Shell middens along our tidal streams and rivers reveal how people here once lived. The story is that shellfish were harvested when food was scarce almost everywhere else. This period of hardship in late winter and early spring was common but part of an annual cycle. As they dug for clams and quahogs in the cold wind, people could see by the height of the sun above the horizon how soon abundance beyond imagining would arrive in the form of migrating fish.

Meeting Grounds

Where two bays or rivers meet and where the ground is level and dry and where beaches offer easy and pleasant spots to launch or disembark from canoes, the people who once inhabited this land met in the fall. Families were reunited and marriages, festivities, trade and games gave people fun things to do. It was a season of plenty and excitement. We can find these meeting grounds still among ballfields and parks near the water or the carefully mowed greenswards of the rich, but the good life is gone that the people who once lived here enjoyed. Life for hunter-gatherers in Maine was once beautiful, challenging and fun.

4. Merrymeeting Bay

Raccoon

The bank was steep and soft, so hauling the boat down the muddy slope was precarious. By the riverside we found we thought a lump of clay tangled among the roots. It gave us just the platform we needed to stand upon while slipping the boat into the current swirling by. But the lump of clay turned out to be a dead raccoon instead. Its body was bloated with gangrene gas and covered all round with silt. All creatures have their place and time and then they die, and even then their remains are useful to someone else, for food perhaps or a place to put one's foot. The cycle of life and death is rapid on this bay. If not a dead raccoon, then a carp's head or wild rice seed floating on the water. Life and death in cycles is the way it is. For those with eyes to see, the drama is what counts. A man who loves this bay needs no more and finds no less.

Mud

To know the bay is to know the mud. In some
places here even the water is just a brown soup,
slightly thinner than the bottom. You can stick
your hand into the water and it will fade from
sight a foot away like a fish slipping below the
surface. On bridges arching over tidal creeks, one
can watch striped bass chase shad or alewives up
and down the channel. One doesn't really see the
fish, just the roiling of the water. Now and then a
silvery flash in the brown below lets you know for
sure. To take a boat out on the bay is to get a
closer look at mud, the smaller the boat the better.
You launch in mud, haul out the boat in mud and
paddle through the mud. You can't always tell out
there when the sky is gray what is mud and what
is water. Contact with the mud follows a
progression. First it gets on your boots, then on
the bottom of the boat. From there it gets on your
paddle, your hands and finally on your face. You
bring the mud back home with you and share it
with those you love. The mud lies beneath all life
that thrives upon this bay. It coats the living and
the dead with silt to show that all are equal here
and all belong. This bay is mud and mud is good.

Feathers

We thought at first they were snowflakes drifting
by on a southwest breeze. Some landed on the
boat and others on our faces. Soon we realized
they were not snowflakes after all, but feathers
drifting in from rafts of ducks and geese. The
birds had landed in stands of wild rice that
morning after flying south all night. There must
have been two thousand of them. Feathers filling
the air like this can happen only where nature is
still wild and free. May the crop of rice on this
bay always be bountiful and may the birds always
return each year. Wild country is best for ducks
and geese but also for wild men like me.

5. Rowing-Sailing Boat

Waves

The waves this afternoon are driven toward land
by a strong onshore breeze. They are steep and
white with foam. Saltwater sprays over the
gunnels of our rowing-sailing craft and brine dries
upon our gear and rowing seats. We row to stay on
course. We row to keep our boat intact. Though
caution is always needed in a boat at sea, the
weather today is special. The wind and waves
make rowing difficult, but this vessel made of oak

and cedar is safe and even quite comfortable.
Thus, as we row across this bay buffeted by wind
and big waves we could not be happier.

Wind

We have taken down the mast and sail. We have
lashed them to the benches. We cannot risk a
sudden gust that hits the sail with full force while
we are perched upon a precipitous wave top. One
blow too hard then and over the vessel might go.
Better to manage the vessel with oars alone. No
luck is needed then, just hard work and vigilance.

Private Place

She was seven years old at the time. Her favorite
spot was a seat in the bow where she could lean
forward and look down into the water or ahead to
the horizon where no other vessels were in sight.
On those calm winter days when the surface of the
sea was so smooth it had the quality of molten
lead, there she sat and pondered. So, we did not
know until many years afterward what our
daughter thought or felt while we rowed in silence
among the islands covered in ice and snow. "I felt
like a bird," she finally said at the age of twenty-
one, "hovering in the air above the water going
wherever I willed. There was only the sound of
the oar blades dipping into the sea and the

creaking of the oarlocks behind me. I was all alone up there in the bow, all alone in my private place. It was pure happiness for me." Parents never know what their children are thinking. How glad we were to learn that years ago our daughter enjoyed our trips in a rowing-sailing boat.

Spray

We were under sail coming back from the islands offshore to the river where we had launched many hours before. It was a warm and sunny summer day with a few white clouds above. We skimmed over the wave crests on a broad reach. The sail was filled with wind. It had a lovely and stylish curve like a bird's wing. The children napped below the rowing seats, the parents manned the tiller and sheet. It was a pleasant run that afternoon, though with our speed we sometimes knocked a wave crest off. Then the spray in the air reminded us that danger was still there.

Surf

We loaded the children into the rowing and sailing boat first, one by one, with a parent to man a set of oars. The biggest and strongest adults held the vessel on either side with water splashing over our knees and thighs. When the nearest breaker was far away, we pushed with all our might and climbed on board. We pulled hard at the oars to increase our speed and reach deep water quickly. All went well until we passed over a bar we had not seen before. A swell upon our beam rose up like a monster from the deep, but chance was on our side. Broadside we rode up and over the curler safely. It's top was thin and clear as glass and then it broke right after that. From then on we kept a careful eye on the sea ahead, for shoals reveal their presence from afar by streaks of foam and turbulence.

Channel

It was a cool day in April when we headed up the bay against the wind. The waves were small but coming fast. Spray came over the side and the ride was a bumpy and tiring one. Two islands nearby with a channel in between offered promise of relief. When we arrived, we felt the wind die down and the water grow calm. The sail was still set on the starboard tack and the wind, though light, pulled us forward slowly through the narrows bounded by trees and rocks. There was not a sound from the mast or sail, not a sound from the hull or shore. Only high above the trees on the island did the wind still roar. Thus, down in the quiet below among the seaweed and the barnacles, making headway against the tide, we ghosted along, delighted and surprised.

31

Maxim

The ocean is vast and beautiful. It is a privilege to row and sail upon its broad expanse, but what the ocean gives it can take away. Use its power wisely and live to row and sail another day.

6. The Harrington

Estuary

A stream flows seaward out of the forest of spruce and fir through salt meadows green as emerald and mudflats glistening in the sun like silver. Near the sea freshwater and saltwater meet and so the water rises and falls in cycles tied to the turning of the moon and earth. Eddies form where currents collide. They turn slowly in circles, bits of sea weed, grass and foam caught in whirlpools drifting up or down stream. Though the Harrington is shallow where it flows through the forest and rises and falls with the tide in the bay, the river never stops flowing or giving life to all those who depend upon it.

Bounty

The daily cycles of the tide attract birds of many kinds. They come in small groups when conditions are right for their method of earning a living. Watch long enough and you will learn who the birds are. Some live in the area all year. Others migrate at this season along the coast. Some are young birds traveling in small flocks learning to make a living on their own. All the birds regardless of their differences have the river in common. They all need to eat and they all share the bounty the Harrington yields.

Rest

The production of food is prolific on the Harrington, more than enough for all. The salt meadows are home to minnows, amphipods and crabs. The mudflats harbor worms and clams. The open water is rich with plankton that feeds a pyramid of smaller and larger fish. It is to this banquet that the birds come and big predators like seals. Mankind has no role here but to watch and listen. He gives nothing to the river that it needs. A wise man understands this and leaves the river and its abundant life alone. The river gives him rest and wonder in return. In a troubled world, who can ask for more?

7. Winter Solstice

Mansions

Along the coast we like early winter best for hiking among the mansions of the rich. The owners are absent this time of year enjoying balmier climates somewhere else. Here the sea at this season is azure blue or sparkling silver in the low light. Long cumulus clouds are pink or purple. The woods are dry and there is as yet but little snow or ice. The grounds of mansions on the coast are not as remote as Labrador or Hudson's Bay, but in winter's silence the forest surrounding them is quite enough to shelter a family of four. We stop to play games on frozen lawns and snack on granite patios. The vistas of the sea are grand. We travel through the grounds of more than one estate on treks of several miles or more. How many depends on their size and the value of the views they provide. We rate the properties on a scale from one to five, noting their good and bad qualities. The rewards for winter hiking among the mansions of the rich are lovely views and practice in the art of invisibility. We take pride in the work we do. We come and go as we please but travel warily, like deer, within the shadows of the trees.

Bay

The row across the bay was long and we arrived at the island just as darkness fell. It was rimmed with ice along the shore and snow lay in patches in the woods. We pushed the boat through the ice to shore and set up camp upon a frozen knoll. A gale from the northwest was expected within twenty-four hours but we needed our rest. The next morning we rose before dawn to examine the sea and sky. Already from the dim light on the horizon we could see whitecaps on the water and hear the wind in the trees. We felt an urge to break camp at once and leave, but we knew that if we left at noon when the tide was slack no current would oppose us and the waves would be smaller. The hours before we launched were anxious ones. We conducted a treasure hunt for the children in the forest and ate our breakfast huddled close to the ground while the wind howled above the trees. It was a relief to load our gear at noon and push out onto the bay at last. No sooner did we leave the island than the sun broke through the clouds. The wind dispersed them into fragments and sunlight reflected off the sea like gold. As the purple shore in the distance to which we rowed came into view, the wind gained speed. But it was coming from the north and we knew that the mountains would shelter the sea from the wind near shore. Soon the water grew calm and we rowed those last few minutes to land in peace. The trip was over and the family was safe, but in our hearts we knew there never was a destination to be reached.

Traveling by Canoe

1. Joy of the Canoe

True Freedom

Three kinds of boats were used before the English invaded this land. There were dugout logs made from the trunks of trees, moose hide boats made from skin wrapped around a wooden frame and birchbark canoes. Here in Maine, the birchbark canoe reigned supreme. It was a long and slender vessel made from wood, sap and bark. Spruce, cedar and white birch trees were needed to build one, for the construction was unique. It resulted in a vessel so versatile and light that no other small boat made then or since has equaled it for traveling about on Maine's rivers and streams. Indeed, the Abenaki traveled by canoe in Maine like birds travel on wings or horses run on long toes and feet. Once you master the art of handling these vessels like the Abenaki did, you know what true freedom means.

Right for You?

Would you like a boat that you can paddle in any direction without making a noise or causing a ripple? Would you like a boat spacious enough to carry gear and two people at least but light enough for one man to carry through the woods or over a mountain? Would you like to stand in this boat in order to fish or to pole upstream through the shallows and rapids? Would you like to use this boat as a shelter on land when it is windy and raining? Would you like a boat that is easy to repair and has no moving parts to break? If your answer is yes to any or all of these questions, then a canoe may be the right boat for you.

Versatility

The people who invented canoes did not feel obliged to make them in only one shape or size. Since they built them one by one as needed they adapted the design to the task at hand. This explains why in written accounts the Abenaki were seen in canoes of all kinds. In general, canoes used on the ocean were longer and wider than those on small ponds and streams. The Abenaki even built very small canoes for use by one person. Even so, in Maine, most canoes shared a similar form and size. That is because they were general purpose designs used mainly on rivers. If you could build a canoe from the materials you found in the forest and had many tasks to perform, wouldn't you do the same thing?

Action

In Midcoast Maine the conditions for travel by canoe are varied, from saltwater bays and large rivers to freshwater ponds, small streams and rapids. It follows that in this region we must choose our boats carefully. Among the many canoes we have tried there are two that suit our needs best. Both are made from modern materials but the form of the hull in each case is an old one. The seventeen footer has a big boat feel, with good glide, stability and momentum. It is superb for long distance travel on saltwater bays or poling up rivers. The fifteen footer accelerates quickly, turns on a dime and is easy to carry. It is the canoe we prefer for use on small streams and ponds or shallow and rocky rapids. We have tried other boats in the past, but they didn't work out, so these two vessels are the survivors of a long and hard selection process. The choice cost us money, time and effort. Like the Abenaki, we know there are no perfect solutions to the problems of traveling by water, but by striving for an ideal we keep busy and every morning we wake up refreshed and ready for action.

2. Poles and Paddles

Poles

Poling a canoe upstream feels like flying though
we are moving only about two miles per hour. The
flow of the current against the hull produces this
heightened sensation of speed. In spite of this
illusion, though, the pole can be used to maneuver
a boat with precision. From eddy to eddy around
the rocks we glide, then up a chute and over a
ledge like a salmon. We push down on the pole
using our weight to achieve the thrust we seek, not
just with our arms and shoulders. On mud the pole
needs a tip shaped like a duck's foot to spread the
load wide on the bottom. On stones the tip should
be metal and pointed for use on hard and slippery
surfaces. The pole can be made of almost any
material we like and the length can be any we
wish. Just be aware that in rapids a pole must be
strong and stiff.

Art of Poling

The key to poling is a number of things, but two
are most important. One, keep the upstream end of
the boat higher than usual, a little above the water
if need be. Conversely, keep the downstream end
lower and deeper. Trim the boat like this whether
going upstream or down for its purpose is to keep

the current from turning the boat sideways. Two, stand at a diagonal facing the pole. That way, when we apply thrust to the pole against the bottom of the river, we can use our weight and the pressure of our feet upon the hull to drive the boat forward while keeping the bow aligned with the current. There are many other skills to learn, of course, like reading the water, using eddies to advantage and snubbing to control the boat's speed when going downstream, but we should learn these two skills first because they lay the foundation for everything else. One thing more to be aware of. If the pole gets stuck in rocks or mud when the current is strong, simply let go and retrieve the pole later. We don't want to toss ourselves out of the boat or tip the boat and our passengers over.

Paddles

A good paddle is like an extension of our body. It should help us to move the canoe forward or backward with a minimum of effort and it should allow us to maneuver the boat by drawing, prying or sweeping as needed. It follows that a paddle's shape, length, balance and weight are all important and that different paddles are designed to handle the boat well under different conditions. To be brief, here is the lesson. For cruising or racing in calm water, a paddle with a bent shaft is best. It creates the least drag in the water and thus mile after mile paddling is easier and faster. In contrast, for waves and whitewater, a paddle with a straight shaft is better. It provides more leverage on the water and both sides of the blade can be used for bracing and power. As for the shape of the blade, this is also important. A long, narrow blade can be useful when the water is deep and calm. During the stroke the narrow blade stays close to the hull, making it easier to keep the boat going straight instead of veering to one side. Conversely, a shorter and wider blade is easier to put in and take out of the water and it provides more power per stroke when needed. Thus, it is better when conditions are difficult or the water is shallow. A paddle should balance about where our lower hand while paddling holds the shaft and every paddle is easier and more pleasant to use when it is light as a feather. Here is the method to determine its length. During a stroke the hand on the top of the paddle should be about equal in height to our shoulder. Longer or shorter than that and it will tire us out. In conclusion, please remember this bit of advice from old-timers. If you think your canoe does not perform well, there are two things you should do before buying a new one. First, adjust the boat's trim to achieve optimal performance. Second, change your paddle. The improvement in the old boat's performance could be dramatic.

3. Tips on Paddling

Whitewater

A canoe allows us to become acquainted with a stream the way we get to know a mountain by hiking. A good canoe for paddling in whitewater rides over the waves like a cork and slips upstream or across the current at our leisure. What we wish to achieve is not speed but control. There is seldom a need to go faster but almost always a need to slow down, back up or go sideways parallel to the current. To achieve these results, the strokes we should master are drawing, prying, bracing and back paddling. We must also learn how and when angling the boat to the current can assist us in moving about easily. As we proceed downstream, our goal is to aim for a route free of obstructions. The way is marked by tongues of deep water called chutes. On the upstream side the chutes appear wide and smooth but downstream they produce waves called haystacks. We should plan ahead to avoid these waves because if they are large they can easily capsize a boat or swamp it. If we make a mistake and turn broadside to the current at any time during our journey, always lean downstream with the paddle blade flat on the water. By sweeping the blade back and forth in a figure eight motion we can keep the boat stable or move it back in line with the current. Never lean upstream for then the pressure on the hull caused by the current will roll the boat over. If we follow this advice and approach every task in life as skillfully as this, then we too can find peace and joy amidst the wild tumult of nature.

Wind

Do you wonder how to keep a canoe on track in a strong wind? The answer is to change the boat's trim. Trim is how the hull sits in the water, whether horizontal or up or down at one end. The key is to move the weight toward the wind using people, gear or jugs of water as ballast. So, when the wind is ahead, move the weight toward the bow. When the wind is behind, move the weight toward the stern. And when the wind is from the side, keep the weight near the center of the vessel. The goal is to keep the end of the canoe facing the wind from being blown sideways while using the rest of the hull like a weathervane to keep the vessel on track. By trimming the hull this way we can paddle a canoe on course across a windy lake or bay for hours. In canoeing as in so many things, knowledge is magic.

Currents

On big rivers as well as life in general, wherever
there is a strong current going one way there is
usually another one going in the opposite
direction. Look for these eddies in coves along the
shore or behind shoals and islands. Then use these
currents to go upstream as far as possible without
making a great effort. From time to time, we must
ferry across the current from one eddy to another.
In Midcoast Maine, however, there is another way
to deal with strong currents. Our rivers are tidal
near the coast, so we can go upstream simply by
waiting until the tide changes. In this case, stay
out of the eddies and keep to the main channel.
The strong flow will carry us twenty or thirty
miles inland if we wish to. Once we reach the
limit of the tide's effect, where the rivers are
smaller, we simply get out our poles and work our
way upstream against the current and the rapids in
the usual manner. It may seem that going
upstream this way defies the rules of logic, but
when traveling by canoe the truth about the world
is never so obvious.

4. Ocean Canoeing

No Matter How Small

We paddled backward as hard as we could when a yacht roared out of the fog and turned in our direction. "Well, this is it," we said to each other, "It appears that they intend to run us over." But when the yacht arrived it slowed down and came alongside. The captain at the wheel surrounded by family and friends looked down from the deck and asked where they were and how to get home again. We had maps and knowledge of the coast, so we described a way for them to get back home as best we could. After that they said thank you and goodbye, then departed with their engines roaring and the water swirling. We paddled on our way as well. Never assume that you cannot be of help, no matter how small you or your boat may be. Knowledge is power, they say. Use it on behalf of all in need.

New World

We knew without seeing how spruce and fir towered above the beach and how the tide split around the headland and swirled alongside. We could even hear the swells breaking in the distance. But not until the fog began to lift did we learn just how beautiful this island could be. From a small circle of blue sky above, sunlight filtered down through the silhouettes of trees. Massive pink ledges arose from shadows along the shore and around the boat wavelets danced and sparkled. At sea as on land patience is a virtue. When the fog lifts, be ready. A new world emerges.

Ironbound Island

For two hundred yards offshore even on a calm day great ocean swells roll in and rebound upon themselves below the cliffs. The collision between the waves and the hard rock makes the sea shake. Small boats passing by vibrate from the energy this surf creates. At a safe distance in our canoe we watch the drama unfold. Clouds come and go, swells roll on, seas slam against the cliffs. We love this drama and its loneliness.

Swells

We are miles from shore on a lovely day, near the outer rim of shoals and ledges that enclose the bay. Paddling is easy in the morning before the onshore breeze arises. We watch the sailboats as they pass by. All their sails are set to catch the wind that is light as breath. When they are gone we are alone again. We ride up and down in the

47

swells, watching and listening. The ocean is full miracles, but only those who are patient discover how much life there is both above and below the surface.

Refuge

We were far offshore on a lovely day in the narrows between islands that were low and barren. Then the water began to stir as schools of fish pursued by giant gray seals crowded the channel. Soon wounded fish and parts of fish rose to the surface while gulls and terns joined the feast from above, shrieking and cawing. We took refuge among the rocks nearby. Like a raft, thick seaweed held the canoe fast and there we waited until the carnage was over.

5. Midcoast Canoe Routes

Old Dams

Most old dams in Midcoast Maine were built for sawing boards or grinding corn or wheat. Today they appear as piles of stone where streams are narrow and steep. Those traveling by canoe should always be wary of these old mill sites. The water in the streams is channeled through the debris in dangerous ways, with blind turns and

narrow chutes blocked by stones and fallen trees.
Best to simply portage around these dams or walk
the boat through the shallows if you have doubt.
We walked our boats through the water swirling
around two old dams on the Pemaquid and then
we portaged a quarter mile around the hard rapids
of a third. Thus, like the Abenaki once did, we
paddled safely down the river to the harbor and
out to sea. Do not think because these old dams
are broken down and the streams are small that
you cannot be drowned in a waterfall.

Carrying Place

Amid the towering pines and spruce in Midcoast
Maine the Abenaki once carried their boats from
bay to bay. The carries saved miles of paddling
around rocky headlands that point like gnarled
fingers into the open sea. We did the same one day
on one old portage route that can still be used. It
begins and ends in shallow coves and so we
arrived at high tide to avoid becoming stranded in
mud or marshes on either side. The old route
follows what is now hayland and pasture and so
the carry was a pleasant one across fields of knee
high grass waving in the wind. We walked in
silence and listened to bluebirds and bobolinks
sing. We were reverent as we passed through
because we know that life is uncertain and that all
we see and love each day is constantly changing.

Whitefield to East Pittston

From the Sheepscot River to the Eastern River there is an ancient carry just over two miles long. The route follows what is now an old road straight as an arrow past suburban homes, alder swamps and beaver ponds. The portage ends on the shore of the Eastern River just below three waterfalls on land that now is posted. The route slices through the hills taking slopes gradually, so the effort to carry a heavy load over this old path in the woods is minimal. The Abenaki designed their carry routes carefully. Like moose and deer who also make their own trails, the Abenaki did not want to work harder than they had to.

Crossroads

Below the village at East Pittston the Eastern River is tidal but freshwater. It flows back and forth among hillsides and wetlands for miles until it merges with Merrymeeting Bay, and Merrymeeting Bay four hundred years ago was a crossroads that people in canoes once used to go anywhere they wished in Maine or New Hampshire. How exciting and beautiful life must have seemed to people who lived in a world without boundaries.

6. What I See and Hear

Mountain Carry

We shoulder our boats with glee and carry them over the mountain. The carry is quite easy to do for the trail is good. Under the great canopy of beech and spruce hardly a shrub or fallen tree trunk blocks the route. It is a mere two miles from shore to shore, but in that distance we travel from the Sheepscot River to the upper St. George. After paddling all day, how good it feels to hike in the woods and use our legs and feet. The forest smells sweet and is quiet and serene. Is this not a relief from the noisy bubbling of a stream?

Spring

Spring is the best time of year in Midcoast Maine for exploring small streams by canoe. No leaves on the trees obscure the view of the forest and the sky is blue and cloudless. In the strong, clear light the gravel and stones beneath the water appear bright amber. The streams make a bubbling noise as they tumble past boulders and tree tops clatter if a wind is blowing. Though we visit only a short time each year, we do not forget how these small streams bring life to the forest and fill us with wonder.

Plant Food Only

Standing high in the canoe on a warm summer day, I see many animals. A beaver flaps his tail and dives. Minnows, bass and pickerel dart into the weeds for cover. Frogs and turtles basking in the sunlight leap into the water. By passing through this wetland I cause trouble for many species though I do not wish to. The canoe moves fast and casts a big shadow. If only these creatures knew how much I loved them. I eat plant food only and the big stick I carry is only for pushing against mud and gravel.

Going My Way

I have come a long way poling up this river and now I sit here resting in the canoe with the pole across my lap. The water is silver and gray under a cloudy sky and I see waves and strong currents moving downstream against me. But I also see eddies going upstream behind rocks and boulders. After all these years it still strikes me as odd and a bit wonderful that we can can find currents going uphill in whitewater. Nature is like that. It can make life hard or it can make life easy, but unlike mankind it has no intent to harm any creature. I am happy on this river and although I am old I still enjoy poling upstream using the eddies.

Wildlife as Neighbors

1. Spring Encounters

Acorn

It was a cool and windy day in May when I first arrived in the oak grove and found no squirrels present. I waited until the sun was low in the west and the forest was shaded, and then to my relief two adults emerged from a den high up in one of the biggest trees. One was a female with lovely gray fur and one was a male with more rusty brown hairs than usual. They were the only gray squirrels I saw that day, yet during the previous autumn the grove was teeming with members of their species. Two more cool days past and then a warm day arrived. To my delight five healthy young squirrels came out of the den to play. They ran up and down the big tree keeping close to their stronghold and avoided the ground. There was one exception, a young female with lovely gray fur like her mother and just once she shinnied down to the bottom of the tree upside down in true squirrel fashion. She then crawled carefully onto an oak root overlooking the forest floor and, gingerly, she put one hand on a leaf while she continued to grasp the root of the tree with her other three paws. I thought she was getting ready to leap onto the forest floor and seek her freedom, but to my amazement she snatched up an acorn under the leaf she was holding and proceeded to eat it like squirrels do, with her tail curling upward behind her and daintily turning the nut over in her paws. When the acorn was finished she still did not venture beyond the safety of the tree. Instead, she raced back up the trunk and joined her siblings playing in the branches high above.

Noon

We were building a bridge across a small stream in the woods when a handsome young rodent that looked like a mouse passed under our feet. He hopped through the sedges and grasses quite ably, but did not show much concern for our presence. Methodically, he turned over the dried stalks of sedges and the brown leaves of maple trees left over from the autumn before and I assumed he was looking for something to eat. At first I was unsure what species he was. Then I saw quite clearly the yellow fur on his flanks, the olive brown stripe down his back and his very long tail. Sure enough, this bold little fellow was a woodland jumping mouse. The species inhabits our eastern forests near streams and wetlands but are seldom observed because they are mainly nocturnal. I also saw that he was quite small even for a male of his species, for the males are smaller than the ladies, generally speaking. So I wondered if the mouse had been born in a litter late last summer. I discussed this hypothesis with the trail crew and noted also that the mouse had colorful fur like the plumage of a warbler. What held my attention most of all, however, was how intent this little creature was on foraging at this time of day, for at that moment the ground was bathed in sunbeams streaming through the spruce and fir. It was May, after all, and not long after members of his kind had come out from their nests and burrows. They hibernate all winter and during that time they do not eat at all. Perhaps this little fellow was so hungry that he was driven to search for food in broad daylight in spite of the risk that other creatures in the forest were watching.

Ford

The doe was scouting the ford between Cow Island and the Topsham shore with her fawn not far behind her. The ford was a gravel bar where the river at low tide pours over the bottom in ripples. The water is so shallow at these times that it is no deeper than our ankles and safe for people and deer to walk through. We were sure that the mother already knew that the ford was there and when to use it, but there was a problem. Three times she led the way across the ford patiently, only to see her fawn rush back to Cow Island after taking a few steps. Although only half her mother's size, the fawn could run and leap gracefully, and she seemed determined to stay on Cow Island playing on the beach much longer. Perhaps the fawn was afraid of the river or what lay on the other side. In any case, after trying three times, the mother conceded to the will of her stubborn child and rejoined her fawn bounding in delight along the sandy shore. We lost sight of the pair when they moved upstream around a bend in the shoreline, so we did not learn when and where they crossed back to the mainland. Even so, as parents ourselves, we surmised that after awhile the mother succeeded in teaching her fawn what needed to be done through patience and kindness.

2. Mice and Voles

Ears and Tails

One should know the difference between mice and voles. Mice are small rodents who leap from place to place if need be in their quest for food and mates. They are very active animals. So, they have big ears to catch the sound from all directions, strong hind legs for jumping and long tails to keep their balance. In contrast, voles are small rodents who scurry close to the ground in their perennial search for food and loved ones. Thus, unlike mice, they have small ears that lie back on their fur out of the way, short legs for running in tight places and short tails because they are not needed for balance. We can safely conclude that the differences in appearance between mice and voles reflects the differences in their way of making a living, but we should keep in mind that both are amazing small mammals who have lived beside us as neighbors for millions of years.

Snow

How animals as small as mice and voles survive the winter is hard to understand until we know the value of snow. Under the snow the temperature of air does not drop below a balmy thirty-two, so mice and voles do very well even on the coldest days and nights of the year. They also build nests, of course, to keep themselves warm and these are vital for protection, but snow is the magic that helps these small creatures survive even the wildest weather.

Praiseworthy

Mice and voles eat different foods in order to share what nature has to offer. Voles, who live close to the ground, eat food high in cellulose like herbs and grasses, although calorie rich foods like seeds and fruit are also welcome. Mice seek food almost always high in calories to suit their more acrobatic way of life, so they prefer seeds, nuts and berries to the extent that they are able to get them. In winter, for example, meadow voles can raise their young in nests beneath the snow because food in the form of grass is plentiful. In contrast, mice must be careful to ration their caches of seeds and nuts that they stored in the fall. Mice and voles may have different strategies for survival, but they both show ingenuity and daring. Indeed, I would say they are quite a bit like us and deserve our admiration.

Memory

How do mice know where their food is stored or where fresh supplies are found in winter? The answer is memory, of course, and this is shown by their tracks in the snow. The tracks go to and from a source of food by a very short route where no wandering is evident. In fact, neurologists say that mice are quite intelligent, just as smart as many species much larger than themselves. Over the years, I have become acquainted with a number of mice who live in the area or in our house, and so I believe what neurologists say is true. The mice I know are wily and persistent little creatures who challenge me daily to outwit them.

3. Moose and Deer

Habitat

Deer and moose do not ask for much, for they are really quite polite. They keep to themselves and like to browse on the twigs of young hardwood trees as well as shrubs, forbs and grasses. It is true that deer like snacking on apples they find on wild trees in the woods or in our farms and orchards, while moose prefer to eat the roots of lily pads they find in shallow ponds and wetlands. Deer thrive best, of course, in hardwood forests while moose do better in forests of spruce and fir. They are both wondrous animals I love to meet, not only because they are very polite but also because they have big brown eyes and long eyelashes.

Grassy Glades

On some Maine islands there are clearings under the spruce and fir where red fescue flourishes as if manicured and small shrubs look as if they have been clipped or sheared. Strange as it may seem, the gardeners here are moose and deer. They visit the islands whenever they wish to enjoy a tasty snack of shrubs or berries and sometimes just for fun or solitude. The moose and deer swim over from the mainland when the weather is pleasant or

else they simply walk across the ice in winter.
Humans are not the only creatures who can solve
a problem. In fact, moose and deer do many
things well when they have time and a reason.

Choice

We were paddling back to shore after spending
one fine November day hiking and taking in the
views on Hog Island. Though the season was late
and the air was cool the day was sunny and
cheerful. No sooner did we approach the mainland
shore when two hikers hailed us. They asked if we
had seen the moose they just observed swimming
in the opposite direction. We regretted to say that
our paths did not cross, but we did confirm that
the moose was headed the right way, for in our
opinion there was no better island to visit on such
a fine day if his purpose was pleasure.

Bay

One day we came across a large buck swimming
across the bay. Naturally, out of courtesy we kept
our distance and did not follow him. It is not
uncommon to see deer traveling out here among
sturgeon, ducks and striped bass. Of course, we
didn't know where this buck was going, but we
guessed that an urge this strong was impelled by
romance or else the allure of some good browsing.

Deer move around like people do to get things done and the bay is quite shallow during much of the tidal cycle, so there are times and places where he could run instead of swim through the water if he wished to. We use a pole to get around when the bay is shallow, but long legs and nimble toes are more versatile considering the many types of ground this wide-ranging buck must bound over.

4. Beaver

Keystone

When I think of animals that are my friends I think of beaver. How can I not sing their praise when they do the world so much good? Consider what they do for other species like invertebrates of all kinds, plus amphibians, fish, mammals and birds, not to mention people in canoes like me. The term ecologists use is keystone species, one that supports an entire way of life by doing something special no other species does. I say let the beaver have the space they need to transform our world into habitat. Today their miracles are needed more than ever and so I pray that there will always be many beaver and that they will always be happy and prosperous.

Little River

How a stream as small as this could be called by
anyone a river is hard to imagine until we know
what the beaver have done. The white man killed
off the beaver to make way for pasture and hay in
the lowlands, but the beaver on the Little River
have come back. Now this tiny trickle of water
has turned into a stream that winds its way
through wetlands of shrubs and trees, flowers and
grasses. It all started from a channel so narrow I
could jump across it in a single leap. The Little
River was once a trickle through the woods, but
from that humble beginning the beaver have
created a new world full of mystery and life.

Chapel

We paddle through a woodland of red maple trees
arching overhead like a chapel, the meadow
beneath green with tussock sedge and grasses.
Even the alders and viburnums by the shore of the
stream have been gnawed down to the level of our
knees and ankles. Thus we pass at ease along this
narrow and winding channel. Beaver are the
builders here for they are the ones who raise the
level of the water. Moose and deer assist by
browsing. This woodland chapel is open for use
by all, a gift by herbivores to all species. Because

of gifts like this, no creature to me is so virtuous as a deer, a moose or a beaver.

Tolls

When we travel by canoe over highways beaver have made, there are times when we must carry our boats in order to pass. Consider this a toll for all the work the beaver have done to make our trip a pleasant one. To pay the toll, we disembark and haul our boats over mounds of sticks and mud. We may stumble in a hole or scratch a leg. Yet, the dams are small and hauling boats over them is not so hard after all. Is this not a small price to pay for the wondrous world the beaver have made?

5. Squirrels

The Grand Three

Three members of the squirrel family in Maine are visible even to homeowners sitting on their porches or driving their autos. One is the grey squirrel, the denizen of hardwood forests. The second is the red squirrel who prefers forests of pine, spruce and fir. The third is the chipmunk who inhabits stony or uneven ground where homes can be found among roots and boulders. All three have different personalities and ways of making a living, so it may take some time to understand why they live where they do and why in some places they are present and in others they are missing. I think that learning about squirrels is good. It leads to wisdom about life in general if we become more loving in the process.

Game

Squirrels of all kinds love to romp and play. During a game, flying squirrels can play by gliding from tree to tree. On the ground they chase each other in circles just like other squirrels do in a mad dash around tree trunks, stumps and boulders. Sometimes it looks as though they are so consumed by excitement that they do not notice that people or predators are watching. But this is not true, for flying squirrels like other intelligent creatures notice a great deal about what is going on in the woods around them. Thus, if a human or predator makes a move they do not like the squirrels stop playing and the game is over.

Chatter

All of Maine's squirrels can make some noise if they wish to but the red squirrel is by far the noisiest of them all. What these furry little creatures lack in size compared to other animals they make up for in ferocity. If they suspect that we are a threat to their cache of seeds in the spruce-fir woods where they live, they will give us a verbal thrashing that we will not soon forget. Even so, the nagging of these furry little animals is not so bad in my opinion compared to the chatter of human beings about business, politics and religion.

Brush Pile

Chipmunks are rare in sand plains where the ground offers few nooks and crannies in which to make a home. But when I left a brush pile in the yard that we manage like an old field, chipmunks moved in. I first saw them watching for danger from the top of the pile and scouting the sticks along the bottom. The pile had lots of nooks and crannies made of small logs and branches. So about a year later I was not surprised when I met a brash young male foraging nearby. Taking a parental role I scolded him soundly for not trying to hide, but inwardly I was pleased that after many years chipmunks had chosen to make our yard their home and become our neighbors.

Rip Rap

Groundhogs are squirrels who live in the ground, and because of their size and weight they are quite good at digging. One day as we passed by a railroad track where rip rap lined the steep hillside, we came across a groundhog who was exceptionally large even by the standards of his species. He was clearly no youngster who would be forced by his mother next spring to seek a home of his own and risk being run over on a busy road or highway. No, this very hefty-looking big male who gazed at us cautiously but without fear, obviously felt safe because of the huge stones he used for a burrow. Robert Frost in his poem noted how important burrows are to this species, but we were impressed even so by how confident this big groundhog could be who had survived so many summers gazing serenely from the walls of his fortress.

6. Woodland Companions

Tracks

We came upon their tracks in the snow only hours after the storm had passed. They were small depressions in the glistening powder made by tails, paws and noses. From this evidence we knew what species were present and what they were doing. Many were familiar, as if we had known them for years as friends and neighbors. Porcupines were foraging among new-fallen trees. White-footed mice were nibbling on the fruit of old flowers. Red squirrels were digging up seeds they had stored in the fall. Deer were browsing in the thickets. Seeing that our friends were still thriving and happy in spite of the cold and snow filled us with joy and eased our worry.

Seldom Seen

Among the mounds of bright green moss covering the rocks and roots of trees one seldom sees the red-backed vole. But one day I came ashore in my canoe and no sooner than I landed and stepped on shore but I caught a glimpse of a furry little rascal darting from one root to another. Yes, indeed, the reddish color on his back was visible. I may have caught him by surprise and no doubt he was fearful and running for his life. I hoped my presence would not cause him fear for long. I wished I could tell him in a way he would understand that I wished him well and would not hurt him.

Hilltops

In Oxford County where small mountains rise from the forest, the ridge tops in winter are highways for shrub and seed eaters. Moose and deer, snowshoe hares and porcupines travel back and forth among the thickets in search of dinner. The things they find to eat are acorns under the snow, fresh bark on trees and nutritious buds on twigs and branches. On these ridges the shrubs are small and the oaks diminutive, but the sun is warm and food is plentiful. I move slowly and sit quietly to avoid disturbing the animals.

Herbivores have excellent manners, so on these hilltops in winter I follow their example.

Restoration

Tunnels in the grass were the first signs we found that meadow voles inhabited our yard. We had stopped scything the lawn only two years before and now the grass in summer was knee high and luxurious. As time passed our yard became a mix of high grass, shrubs and small trees, so now it provides breeding habitat not only for meadow voles but for eight other species of small mammals and three species of small birds. Many invertebrates like crickets, grasshoppers and butterflies have also joined us who never lived here before, not to mention occasional visitors like turkey and deer. How glad we are to witness this transformation and repay Maine's wildlife in a small way for all the joy they have given us.

South of Bangor

1. Suburbs

Country Charm

To a geographer, the suburbs in southern Maine
represent a new type of city, one with a dispersed
form based on travel by automobile and highways.
Suburbs merge from all directions to form cities
among the trees millions of square miles in extent.
Some undeveloped land persists nonetheless,
conserved by the ingenuity of land trusts. The
parcels of protected land on a map look like
shards of broken glass, but on the ground the
woodlands and fields among the homes add
country charm. The people who live in these
suburbs want to believe they are like old Mainers,
able to endure whatever hardships nature throws
in their way. They celebrate this myth by getting
out their chain saws in the fall to cut firewood and
planting gardens in the spring. Mankind has a
penchant for making things up but sawing wood
and gardening are not the worst rituals he has used
to blind himself to truth. As for me, though I love
the trees in Maine, I know all too well the urban
sprawl they shield from view.

Highest and Best Use

In reaction to wetland conservation laws developers say there is a wetland behind every tree. I say in reaction to development that buildings and roads in Maine multiply like flies on a carcass, for surely nature in Maine is dying. My neighbors do not seem to notice, for each generation only knows what it sees, and, since over time wild nature is fading away, the standard of what is wild or not grows steadily smaller. Would my neighbors think differently if they traveled on foot or by canoe over the land and waters of the state like I do? I think not. From their point of view there is plenty of real estate left among the nooks and crannies of suburbs and highways. Remember, to Americans nature means money, not freedom, so as long as there are lawns and trees among the buildings to keep things green and profits keep rolling in they are happy.

Fragments

A free flowing river rises and falls with snowmelt and rain. Sometimes the water in the channel is deep and sometimes it is shallow, but fish can come and go as they please and wildlife is abundant. My countrymen, however, do not approve of rivers behaving this way. Instead, they insist that every river and stream be dammed not once but many times over if need be. Their reasons for blocking up rivers are legion, but the two most common today are to generate electric power and to create lakes and ponds where the shorelines are good for development. The impoundments created by the dams are often clouded by algae or filled with invasive species. Even the fish may have to be stocked. Nonetheless, on these crowded waterways people have a wonderful time racing back and forth in motorboats or chatting with their friends and neighbors on shore. In a desperate attempt to find evidence that wild nature still exists, I travel by canoe to the fragments of free flowing rivers and streams that are left. They are few and far between and I must travel a great deal to visit them. When I arrive I gaze in awe and silence at what is there. What I see appears to be wild, but missing are the migratory fish that swim in the from the ocean to spawn and all the other wildlife that the presence of the fish make possible. I pray that someday mankind will change his ways and let rivers flow free again, but my hopes are far-fetched. Man's view of the world is very small. To him wild nature makes no sense until it has been transformed into something else he thinks is more useful, no matter how trivial.

2. Origins

Property Rights

The conquest of Maine by the English was led by groups of wealthy proprietors. They were armed with deeds granted by the government in Boston and, in order to profit from rents and fees, they invited lower class men and their families to settle in Maine and develop it. But on the frontier things did not go as the proprietors planned. Many went bankrupt and in the confusion the settlers grabbed all the land they could get. If agents arrived from Boston to enforce a deed, the settlers drove them out at gunpoint if they had to. Thus arose the libertarian ideal that still inspires my neighbors. When government is weak, so the argument goes, we are all equal in our chances to get rich by ravaging nature.

Clearing the Land

The goal in colonial times was to conquer Maine without war if possible, for it was much easier and cheaper to do so. The indigenous people were hunter-gatherers and so the forests and waterways in their natural state provided all the food and materials for life that the indigenous people needed. It followed that to defeat the hunter-gatherers and drive them out all one had to do was to destroy wild nature. By cutting down the forests, turning over the soil, damming the rivers and killing the wildlife, no food or shelter or building materials of any kind were left for indigenous people to live on. The wars we hear so much about were simply the outbreaks of violence that occurred from time to time when Maine's indigenous people grew desperate and fought for survival.

3. East and West Branch

Confluence

Two branches of the Cathance River converge in a plain just west of Bowdoinham. Here the West Branch and the East Branch meet to form the main stem, a stream winding its way among low hills covered with pastures, fields and woods. This landscape was created by man for grassland farming. The products are cattle, hay and timber. All landscapes created by man are based on money. Let the demand for lean, grass fed beef go down and say good bye to this forgotten world of fields and woods. Houses and roads will take their place.

Flood

March is a good time to visit the valley where the
West Branch and the East Branch meet. Melting
snow and pelting rain under the cloudy skies of
spring engorge the streams. Where the streams
meet here below Doughty Road they overflow
across a half wild plain crisscrossed by wire
fences and black willow. In summer cattle roam
here at will amidst flowers and luxuriant grass,
but a cow or a man stranded here now would
drown in the flood. Come to this valley in March
and learn what this landscape has to teach. The
gurgling of the eddies behind the trees and fence
posts tells us this land is not our own to keep.

Lives or Dies

We hear in the distance the din of chippers
grinding up slash and the growl of trucks hauling
away logs. The building of suburbs never stops.
Yet here in this valley for one moment more all is
still. A hawk soars overhead and turkeys probe for
insects in the grass. We hear a breeze blowing
through the forest and the river flowing past. It is
a calm and peaceful day here like many we have
known. Yet our love does not decide whether this
valley lives or dies, but only market forces.

Gary Fogg earned a Bachelors of Arts degree in English from Bates College and a Masters degree in Landscape Architecture from the University of Massachusetts Amherst. After many years working at odd jobs while he travelled about in the Maine woods, he started his own land use planning firm under the name of Land and People, LLC. For twenty years as a planning consultant he helped to conserve land and protect the environment in southern Maine. Gary is now retired and lives in Topsham. Besides canoeing and hiking, he performs trail work for the Brunswick-Topsham Land Trust and continues to write about nature and history.